Poisoning

Dr. Alvin Silverstein,

Virginia Silverstein, and

Laura Silverstein Nunn

My Health
Franklin Watts

A Division of Scholastic Inc.

New York • Toronto • London • Auckland • Sydney

Mexico City • New Delhi • Hong Kong

Photographs © 2002: Dembinsky Photo Assoc.: 20 (Marilyn Kazmers), 6, 22 (Patti McConville), 33 (Mark J. Thomas); Peter Arnold Inc.: 11 (Manfred Kage), 7 (Leonard Lessin), 19 (Kevin Schafer); Photo Researchers, NY: 30, 32 (Scott Camazine), 12 (David Gifford/Science Photo Library), 10 (Jim W. Grace), 27 (Tom McHugh), 31 (Larry Miller), 25 (Richard Phelps Frieman), 18 (Andrew Syred/Science Photo Library); PhotoEdit: 4 (Richard Lord), 34 (Cathy Melloan), 17, 23 (David Young-Wolff); Stock Boston/Liane Enkelis: 15; The Image Works/Townsend P. Dickinson: 35; Visuals Unlimited: 14 (Eric Anderson), 24 (RDF), 37 (David Sieren), 9 (George J. Wilder), 16 (David Wrobel).

Cartoons by Rick Stromoski

Library of Congress Cataloging-in-Publication Data

Silverstein, Alvin.
    Poisoning / by Dr. Alvin Silverstein, Virginia Silverstein, and Laura Silverstein Nunn.
        p. (cm).—(My Health)
    Includes bibliographical references and index.
    Contents: Beware of poisons — What is poison? — Poisons you eat or drink — Poisons in the air — Poisonous animals — Poisonous plants — First aid treatment.
    ISBN 0-531-12194-1 (lib. bdg.)   0-531-16240-0 (pbk.)
    1. Poisoning—Juvenile literature. [1. Poisoning.] I. Silverstein, Virginia B. II. Nunn, Laura Silverstein. III. Title. IV. Series.
RA1214.S54 2003
615.9—dc21   2002001729

Contents

Beware of Poisons

When you were very young, you probably liked to explore and check things out, just like any curious toddler. But when you wandered over to the cabinet containing detergents, floor cleaners, and other household products, your mom or dad probably ran over to you, picked you up, and told you, "No!"

Your parents weren't trying to ruin your fun. They were just trying to protect you from the harmful poisons in the cabinet. Many household products, especially cleaners, contain poisonous chemicals that can make you really sick if they get into your body.

By now, you are old enough to know that it is dangerous to drink from a bottle of drain cleaner or gulp down pills from the medicine cabinet. But there are

Did You Know...

Poisonous products often come in pretty colors and appealing containers. Sometimes they even smell sweet. That's why young children may mistake them for something good to eat or drink.

◀ **Cleaners can be very dangerous and should be kept away from children.**

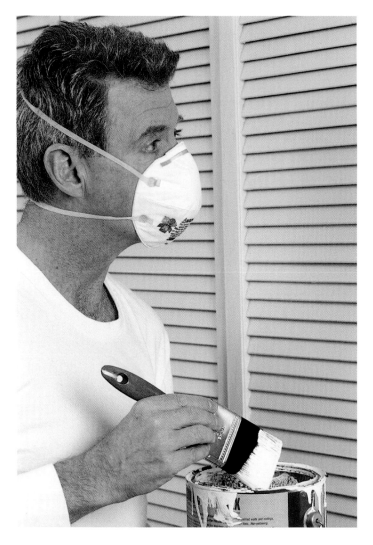

still **poisons** that kids your age and even grown-ups have to watch out for. They are not all packaged in boxes and bottles. Certain plants contain poisons that may harm you if you eat them or even touch them. Wasps, snakes, and other creatures use their poisons to defend themselves and may sting or bite you if they feel threatened. Breathing in fumes from paint, gasoline, or glue can make you very sick. Even food can turn poisonous if it is not stored or cooked properly.

Wearing a mask while you paint can protect you from poisonous fumes.

How much do you know about poisons? Would you know what to do in a poisoning emergency? Fortunately, there are many things you can do to stay safe. In this book, you will learn more about poisons and what to do if someone has been hurt by them.

What Is a Poison?

Have you ever seen any products around your house with the word **toxic** on the label? Toxic is just another word for poisonous.

A poison or toxin is a substance that can cause sickness or death if it gets into or on the body. There are a number of ways that this can happen. Poisons may be swallowed when someone eats or drinks something that is toxic. Poisons can also enter the body through the nose or mouth when a person breathes. The eyes are another entry point into the body. Liquids that splash into a person's eyes may pass through the eyes' thin, moist covering and get into the blood. Some poisons can get into the body through the skin. This can happen easily if a person has a cut or scrape, but some

Many household cleaners use warning labels to alert users to the poisons inside.

Form of Poison	Common Examples
Solids	Medicine (pills, tablets, capsules), plants, detergents, and fertilizers
Liquids	Lotions, liquid laundry soap, floor cleaner, furniture polish, lighter fluid, and syrup medicines
Sprays	Pesticides, spray paint, and aerosol sprays
Gases or Vapors	Paint or gasoline fumes, fumes from car exhaust, fumes from gas or oil-burning stoves, cigarette smoke, and air pollution

poisons can soak right through unbroken skin. Other poisons can cause a rash or some other harmful effect when they get on the skin.

Some poisons can cause great harm in very tiny amounts. Others are less harmful, and their effects depend on how much of them get into the body. Small doses may cause little or no harm at all. In fact, some toxins are actually helpful in small amounts and may be used as medicines. But large amounts of those same toxins can cause serious health problems if they get into the body. Small doses of poison, when taken repeatedly, may also be harmful. That's because they build up in the body and may eventually damage important organs.

A Helpful Poison

One of the deadliest poisons of all is botulinum toxin, made by the **bacteria** that cause the most dangerous form of food poisoning, **botulism**. But doctors use this toxin in a form called Botox to safely treat various muscle problems, such as uncontrollable twitching in an eyelid, arm, or leg. Injecting a tiny amount of Botox blocks the messages going from the nerves to the muscles and stops the twitching. When injected into the muscles of the face, Botox can smooth out wrinkles—but the effects last only a few months.

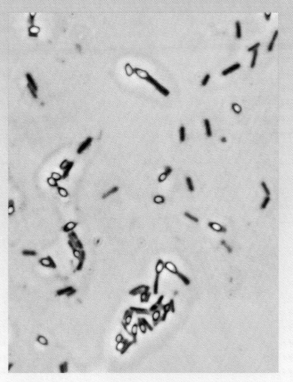

The bacteria that causes botulism can be very dangerous.

Fortunately, your body has built-in defenses to protect you from poisons and other foreign substances. For example, your skin is like a suit of armor that normally helps to keep out harmful things that come in contact with your body. Your nose contains bristly hairs to filter out some of the particles from the air you **inhale** (breathe in). Any particles that get past these hairs get stuck in a pool of gooey **mucus**.

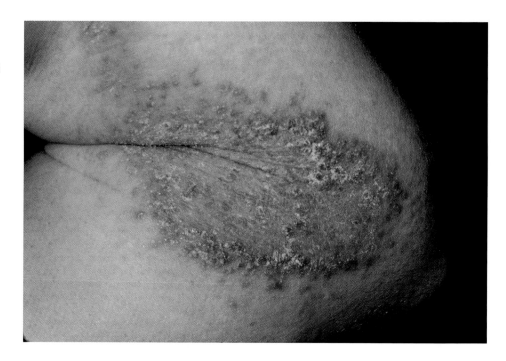

But poisons that get past the first line of defense can damage body tissues and important organs. Touching the leaves of the poison ivy plant, for example, can give you a rash because irritating oils rub off onto your skin. If a poison gets into your eyes, it may cause burns, blisters, or even blindness.

When you swallow a poison, it may burn your mouth, throat, and **esophagus** (the tube that connects your mouth to your stomach). The poison may irritate the stomach lining, too, and your body will try to get rid of it quickly. Damaged cells in the stomach lining let out chemicals that call for help.

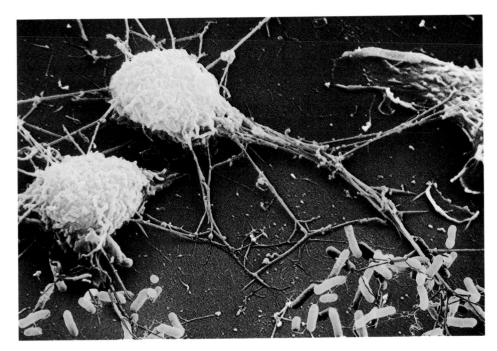

Two white blood cells are attacking some *E. coli* bacteria.

Cells in the area get swollen and leaky, producing **inflammation**. You feel uncomfortable, but this swelling helps **white blood cells**, the body's roaming defenders, to move in the area. They get to work killing germs and cleaning up the damage. Meanwhile, the muscles in the stomach wall start to **contract** (tighten) so much that it hurts. Messages are sent to a special **vomiting** center in your brain. As the stomach contractions get stronger, the valve at the top of the stomach pops open, and you throw up. Whatever you swallowed goes gushing up through the esophagus and out your mouth.

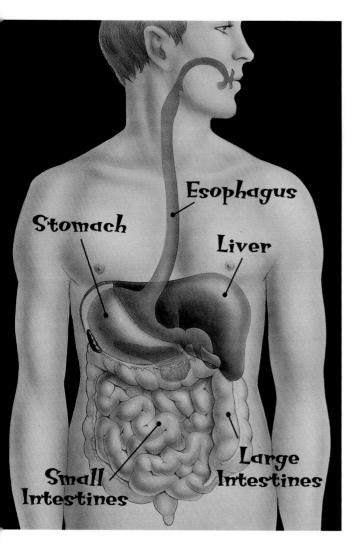

Esophagus

Stomach

Liver

Small Intestines

Large Intestines

This diagram shows the organs of the digestive system.

The contractions from the stomach may also spread down into your small intestine, the coiled tube where food materials are **digested**, or broken down into nutrients the body can use. You may feel these contractions as painful cramps, but they are helping to get rid of the poison by moving partly digested food along much faster than usual. You may get a sudden urge to go to the bathroom, and when you do, your stools (body wastes) are soft or even liquid. You have **diarrhea**. The stools are watery because the wastes did not spend much time in your large intestine, where excess water is normally removed.

An important organ that defends the body against poisons is the liver, a large organ that changes things chemically to make them less poisonous. But the liver itself may become damaged if it is constantly being exposed to poisons. It is made up of living cells that poisons can damage. Fortunately, the body can replace damaged liver cells unless too many of them are damaged in a short time.

The kidneys may also be damaged by poisons. Their job is to take waste products out of the blood, along with water to wash the waste products away. The mixture of waste and water is called **urine**. While making urine, the kidneys come into contact with the poisons your body is trying to get rid of. These poisons may harm some of the kidney cells. If many kidney cells are damaged, these organs cannot do their job properly and waste products build up. Poisons may stay in the blood and travel to other organs, damaging them as well.

The kidneys produce urine constantly, but you go to the bathroom only a few times a day. Between your trips to the bathroom, urine is stored in a baglike organ called the **bladder**. For hours at a time, the bladder is exposed to poisons in the urine, so it, too, may be damaged by them.

Poisons You Eat or Drink

You come home from school and grab an apple from the refrigerator. Don't forget to wash it first! Most fruits and vegetables are sprayed with **pesticides**, poisonous chemicals that farmers use to get rid of insects and other pests that can harm their crops.

Always wash fruits and vegetables before you eat them.

14

It is important to wash fruits and vegetables before eating them so that these poisons don't get into your body.

Eating just one apple without washing it will not harm you. It probably contains only small traces of pesticides. But if you never wash the foods you eat, poisons may build up in your body. It may take years, but eventually they could damage important organs.

Lawmakers are passing rules and regulations that will make pesticide use safer. Government inspectors check foods to make sure they are safe to eat. Chemical companies are also developing pesticides that are less toxic to humans and the environment.

Meanwhile, some people are turning to **organic foods**. Organic foods are grown "naturally" without the use of pesticides or chemicals of any kind. Many people

Many organic foods can be found in your grocery store.

believe that these products are not only safer, but also better for the environment.

Even if you're eating organic food, that doesn't mean you don't have to wash it. Beef and poultry, whether organic or not, may carry germs that can cause **food poisoning**. Food poisoning is an illness caused by eating food that contains certain kinds of microscopic creatures that live and grow inside the body. Food that has been in contact with something bad or harmful is said to be **contaminated**. Foods can become contaminated when bacteria grow and multiply, especially in food that has been left at room temperature too long. Bacteria can be killed when they are exposed to very hot temperatures. Cold temperatures, such as those in a refrigerator or freezer, keep them from growing and multiplying actively.

Never leave meats or dairy products out of the refrigerator for very long.

Salmonella is a kind of bacteria that can cause food poisoning. Salmonella is found mostly in raw and undercooked eggs, poultry, meat, and milk products. Bacteria from these foods can settle in the small intestine and multiply. They produce a toxin that can damage or kill body cells. When enough cells are harmed (usually within six to forty-eight hours after exposure) symptoms start to develop. They may include fever, headache, diarrhea, nausea, vomiting, and even death in serious cases. That's why it is very important to cook eggs, poultry, and meat completely to kill any *Salmonella* bacteria they may contain. You should always wash your hands after touching raw meat or poultry. Otherwise, the bacteria could get into your body if you touch your eyes, nose, or mouth.

Always wash your hands after handling raw meat.

Multiplying by Dividing

When bacteria get inside your body, they can multiply quickly. Each bacterium reproduces by dividing into two smaller bacteria. Each one grows until it is ready to divide too. When the temperature is just right and there is plenty of food, one bacterium can divide into two bacteria every twenty to thirty minutes. After a few hours, just one germ could multiply into millions!

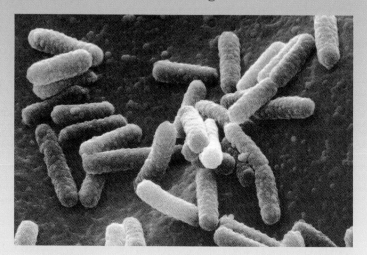

Bacteria multiply very quickly.

Food manufacturers use various methods to keep foods free of harmful germs or to prevent them from multiplying. Milk is **pasteurized** (heated to a very high temperature and then cooled quickly) to kill bacteria. Deep freezing and drying foods stops the growth of germs. Canned foods can be kept safely for a long time because most bacteria cannot grow and multiply without air. But the deadliest form of food poisoning, botulism, is caused by a type of bacterium that can grow without air. Normally, bacteria are killed by the heat and high pressures of the canning process. If canning is not done properly, however, they can grow and multiply and produce a very deadly toxin.

Fortunately, botulism is rare in the United States. Symptoms of botulism are blurred or double vision, weak or tired feeling, and difficulty swallowing. It may result in death if it is not treated right away. Protect yourself by throwing out any bulging or swollen cans in your home. Bulging, which may be a sign of botulism, is caused by a buildup of gas produced by the growing bacteria.

What's that gray, fuzzy-looking stuff that grows on foods left in the refrigerator too long? It's mold caused by **fungi**, and it may be poisonous. Unlike most bacteria, fungi can live in very hot or cold environments.

Some molds can be poisonous to eat.

Poisonous Puffer

The puffer, also called the blowfish, is one of the most poisonous sea creatures, but some people like to eat it. This fish is famous for blowing itself up like a balloon when it is frightened. It carries a deadly poison in certain parts of its body. In Japan, specially trained cooks prepare puffer for eating by taking out the liver and other poisonous parts. The rest of the fish is safe to eat.

That's why refrigerating food may keep bacteria from growing, but it won't keep mold from growing. So if you see strange-looking stuff growing on the leftovers, don't try it. Just remember: when in doubt, throw it out!

Lots of people have to take headache or cold medicine every once in while. Medicines help you feel better when you're sick. But you're only supposed to take a certain amount. If you take too much of a drug, it can be more harmful than helpful. Never take more than the dose stated on the label, and never take medicine that was prescribed for someone else.

What is good for someone else may be wrong for you. For example, the right dose of medicine for an adult may be too large for a child.

There is one poison that many people drink on purpose. The alcohol in beer, wine, and hard liquor can have powerful effects on the body. Small amounts of alcohol may act on the brain to make a person feel relaxed and happy. But even small amounts can also have bad effects on coordination and judgment. Driving a car or cutting with a sharp knife could be dangerous after drinking alcohol. Larger amounts of alcohol can damage organs such as the liver, and very large amounts can even cause death. Some people may become **addicted** to alcohol. They feel the need to drink it even when they know it is not good for them. Laws that set a minimum age for drinking alcohol (usually from eighteen to twenty-one) are designed to protect children from its harmful effects.

Poisons in the Air

Have you ever been in a room that has just been painted? It was probably so smelly that you had to leave the room. Many paints and varnishes contain poisonous chemicals that are sent into the air in the form of invisible gasses or fumes. They may get into your body when you breathe or inhale. After a while, you may feel dizzy, get a headache, or feel sick to your stomach. It's always a good idea to open up the windows when you're in a room that contains fresh paint.

Always open a window when you smell paint fumes.

Many household products, such as ammonia, bleach, and other cleaners, also contain chemicals that can make you sick when you inhale them. The toxins in bleach, for example, are so strong that inhaling them for just a short time can damage cells in your nose and throat. They become inflamed, and extra mucus is produced, giving you a runny nose, sore throat, and cough. The fumes may also make your eyes red and watery. Adding water to such strong cleaning products before using them can help to lessen the effects of the toxins.

The poisons in bleach can harm your airways if they are inhaled for even a short time.

Glues and cements, such as those used in making toy models, can also give off toxic fumes. Some kids try sniffing glue because it makes them feel good. But the chemicals in glue, like the alcohol in beer or wine, can damage the brain, liver, and other important organs. Some kids have even died after sniffing glue.

You can usually smell paint fumes and can tell when a room has been cleaned with powerful cleaners, but not all airborne poisons can be detected easily. Carbon monoxide, for instance, is a poisonous gas that is invisible and has no odor, so you don't know when it is present. You may get carbon monoxide poisoning if you are exposed to a faulty heater or other appliance, or breathe in car exhaust fumes, which may get into your house if you have an attached garage. This gas is very dangerous because it can damage the red blood cells and keep them from carrying oxygen to your body cells. Early symptoms may include headaches, vision problems, dizziness, sleepiness, ringing in the ears, nausea, and vomiting. If the problem is not treated early on, death may result. Protect yourself with carbon monoxide detectors.

A carbon monoxide detector can warn you if the poisonous gas is in your house.

These devices can warn you if there are any traces of the poisonous gas in the air.

Cigarette smoking, like drinking alcohol, is another example of people taking poisonous substances on purpose. Cigarettes contain hundreds of poisonous chemicals that are sent into the body when a person smokes a cigarette. These poisons damage body cells as they go down the throat, through the airways,

The poisons in cigarette smoke can severely damage a person's airways.

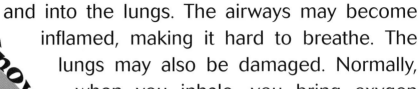

Children who live with a parent who smokes are sick more often than children whose homes are free of "secondhand smoke."

and into the lungs. The airways may become inflamed, making it hard to breathe. The lungs may also be damaged. Normally, when you inhale, you bring oxygen from the air into your lungs. Oxygen passes into the blood and is then carried to the body cells and used for energy. But when the toxins in cigarette smoke damage the lungs, serious breathing problems develop. In addition, many poisons in cigarette smoke can cause cancer of the mouth, throat, and lungs.

When a smoker takes a puff and then **exhales** (breathes out), poisonous chemicals are sent out into the air. Everyone around the smoker breathes in these poisons too. Inhaling somebody else's smoke can give you the same kinds of health problems that smokers develop.

Poisonous Animals

Many animals use poisons to defend themselves or to catch or kill their prey. Poisonous snakes, for example, have **fangs**, which are long, hollow teeth that can inject **venom** (poison) when they bite. A snake uses its venom to makes its prey weak and helpless. After the quick-acting poison has done its job, the snake swallows its prey whole. Snakes also bite animals that are attacking or threatening them. A person who accidentally steps on a snake or goes near one is likely to be bitten. A bite from a poisonous snake can make a person very sick or even die.

Fortunately, most snakes are harmless. Most poisonous snake bites in the

A rattlesnake uses its fangs to inject poison into its victim.

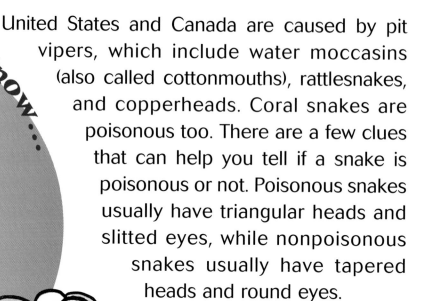

The spitting cobra of southern Africa squirts venom through its fangs into its victim's eyes. It can hit a target 7 feet (2 meters) away!

United States and Canada are caused by pit vipers, which include water moccasins (also called cottonmouths), rattlesnakes, and copperheads. Coral snakes are poisonous too. There are a few clues that can help you tell if a snake is poisonous or not. Poisonous snakes usually have triangular heads and slitted eyes, while nonpoisonous snakes usually have tapered heads and round eyes.

The venom of rattlesnakes and copperheads attacks blood cells and the **tiny blood vessels** through which blood flows. Blood leaks out of the damaged blood vessels instead of traveling through the body and delivering oxygen and nutrients to cells. The victim becomes weak, confused and faint. The venom of coral snakes and cobras attacks the nerves and causes numbness, weakness, twitching, and breathing problems.

Activity 1: Make Your Own Splint

If you are bitten by a snake, it is important to keep the venom from spreading from the area of the bite to other parts of your body. Keeping as still as possible can help because when you move around, your muscles help to pump blood throughout your body. If you have a bite on an arm or leg, you can make a splint to keep that part of the body still. Various things you can find around the house can be used to make a splint.

Try making a practice splint so you will know how to do it quickly in case you have a bite emergency. For this activity, you'll need something stiff and firm to keep the arm or leg straight, such as rolled-up newspapers or magazines, a ruler, or an umbrella. You'll also need something to wrap around the framework of the splint to hold it in place. You can use string, belts, tape, a roll of gauze, backpack straps, or the long sleeves of a shirt. You may need someone to help you to put a splint on your arm. Splints are good first aid for spider bites, broken bones, and sprains.

Many people are afraid of tarantulas because of these spiders' large size—up to 2 inches (52 mm) in body length. But the venom of tarantulas is not very strong. In fact, their bites are no more harmful to people than is a bee sting.

Only two spiders in the United States have venom strong enough to kill a person: the black widow and the brown recluse. Both spiders are found mainly in the southern states.

Female black widow spiders are poisonous.

Black widows spin their webs around wood piles, stone walls, and other quiet, outdoor places. Only females have venom. The female spends most of her time hanging upside down on her web, waiting for insects, spiders, and centipedes to get caught on its sticky strands. You can recognize her by the red hourglass marking on her belly. Black widows don't attack people, but if you touch them, they will bite to defend themselves. Their venom attacks the nerves and can make a person very ill, but victims usually recover within a week.

A brown recluse spider may defend itself with a bite when disturbed.

The brown recluse spider is found outdoors in piles of rocks, wood, or leaves, or indoors hanging out in dark closets, attics, or basements. It has a brown body and a violin-shaped mark on the back of its head. Like black widows, these spiders do not usually attack, but will defend themselves if they are disturbed. Their venom destroys blood cells and tissues around the bite. Although they can make a person feel very sick, brown recluse bites are rarely deadly.

Not all poisonous animals inject their venom with fangs. Bees and wasps have poisonous stingers at the ends of their bodies. The best-known wasps are hornets and yellow jackets. A wasp has a reusable stinger and

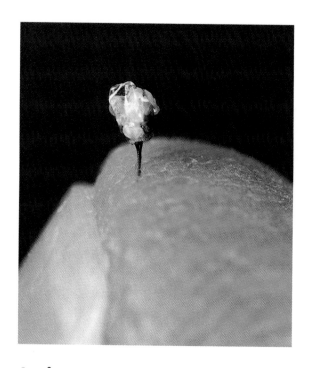

A stinger can still release poison even after the bee is gone.

can sting many times. A bee, however, leaves its stinger in the skin. The stinger, which contains the venom sac, continues to pump out venom even after the bee has gone. The longer it is left in, the more the sting will hurt. So the stinger should be removed carefully as soon as possible. Bee or wasp stings are painful, but they are not dangerous unless you get stung many times or you are allergic to the venom.

Jellyfish are armed with thousands of poison darts in their tentacles. When an object brushes against its tentacles, the jellyfish fires its stinging poison into the victim. This is how a jellyfish catches its prey, but it will also sting a person who brushes against it. Most jellyfish stings are not dangerous to people, but they are very painful. A jellyfish sting may give you a painful, burning feeling, and a bumpy, red rash may develop. Never touch a dried-out jellyfish or broken-off tentacles—they can still sting you.

Certain types of frogs that live in the tropical regions have poison stored in glands in their skin. These frogs

are usually colored red, blue, yellow, or orange. Their bright colors act as a warning to predators that say, "Don't eat me! I'm poisonous!" Any animal that tries to eat the poisonous frog will get sick or die. If the animal survives, it is not likely to bother brightly colored frogs in the future.

Most poisonous frogs are not harmful to people. An open scratch or cut, however, may allow poison to get into the body and cause a painful reaction. South American natives put the toxins from poisonous frogs on the tips of the arrows they use for hunting. Today, surgeons use one of these toxins while they are operating to paralyze a patient's muscles temporarily.

Poisonous Plants

Some plants produce poisons to protect themselves against animals that try to eat them. A caterpillar or snail that feeds on such a plant will not get a second chance to do so. These poisonous plants can also be harmful to people. Some of them can make you really sick if you eat them. Others contain substances that irritate the skin, and touching the plant can cause an itchy rash.

It may be tempting to eat the pretty red berries growing on the bushes in your backyard, but don't—they could be poisonous. Some common plants that

It is very important to identify a plant before you touch it.

produce poisonous berries include yew, mistletoe, jasmine, and holly. Yew and holly also have poisonous leaves, as do a number of other plants.

Some wild mushrooms contain deadly poisons. Of course, the ones you buy at the supermarket are safe, but never eat mushrooms that you find growing in your backyard. Only mushroom experts can tell which mushrooms are poisonous. Mushroom poisoning does not make a person sick right away. Symptoms may not develop until twelve to twenty-four hours later. By then, it will be too late to vomit to rid the body

of the poisons. The delay in the development of symptoms also may cause a person to eat more of the mushrooms, thinking they are harmless.

Have you ever gotten an itchy rash after touching a poison ivy plant? As many as 80 to 90 percent of people are likely to have an allergic reaction to the sticky oil of the poison ivy plant and its relatives, poison oak and poison

Every part of a poison ivy plant is dangerous.

Burning poison ivy plants is dangerous. Some of the irritating oil may get into the smoke. If this smoke is inhaled, it makes the lining of a person's nose, breathing tubes, and lungs swell up and the person can't breathe.

sumac. The poison can be found in all parts of the plant: leaves, stems, roots, flowers, and fruits. Even if you didn't touch the plant directly, you can get a rash from patting a dog, touching a friend, or picking up a baseball that had touched the poisonous plant. Poison ivy causes redness and itchy, oozing blisters on the skin.

Poison ivy usually grows as a vine and climbs on trees, rocks, and walls. It also spreads over the ground when there's nothing to climb. You can avoid poison ivy by following the popular saying, "Leaflets three, let them be." Poison ivy has shiny leaves in groups of three. The leaves may come in different shapes: wide, narrow, smooth edged, and jagged edged. In the summer, the plant produces small, greenish-white flowers and white berries.

Poison oak looks different from poison ivy. It got its name because its leaves look somewhat like those of an oak tree, although the two are not related. Poison oak is a low, bushy plant, that has leaves in groups of three, like poison ivy. The leaves are thick and leathery, with a dark green color on top and a lighter color underneath. The poison oak plant has yellow-green flowers and white berries.

Poison sumac is not as common as its poisonous relatives. This plant is a tall, skinny shrub or tree with groups of seven to thirteen smooth-edged leaves and white berries. It grows in wet places, such as in swamps and on the banks of streams. Poison sumac contains more poison in its sap than does poison ivy and poison oak, so touching it can cause a much more serious skin rash.

Poison oak has clusters of three leaves and grows low to the ground.

First Aid Treatment

You're helping out with the household chores. You try to spray the glass cleaner on the windows, but the nozzle is facing the wrong way. The fluid sprays into your eyes! What do you do?

While playing in the backyard with your little sister, you notice that she is munching on some wild mushrooms. You don't know if these mushrooms are poisonous. Whom should you call?

By now you know that poisons come in many different forms, and many of them can be found in your own home. The more you learn about poisons and where they are found, the better chance you have of avoiding them. Not only can you keep yourself safe from poisons, you can help to keep others safe, too.

If you find yourself in an emergency situation, tell a grown-up right away. While you're waiting for help, there are some things you can do on your own.

Kind of Emergency	What to do While You're Waiting
Swallowed drugs or chemicals	After checking a poison control center, syrup of ipecac may be used to cause vomiting. Drinking activated charcoal mixed with water can help keep chemicals from getting into the blood.
Food poisoning	Drink a lot of fluids to replace what is lost through vomiting and diarrhea. See a doctor if stomach pains and diarrhea continue for more than a day or so, or if there is blood in the vomit or stools.
Splashed chemicals into eyes	Wash eyes with a lot of water when splashed with cleaning products or other irritating chemicals. Do not rub eyes.
Skin irritation or burns from chemicals or plants	Wash thoroughly with cool water. Remove any contaminated clothing or jewelry and wash thoroughly before wearing again.
Spider bite	Ice the area and keep it still. When talking to the doctor, describe the spider if possible.
Snakebite	Do not ice the area (this may damage the skin). When talking to the doctor, describe the snake if possible. Even nonpoisonous snakebites should be looked at because they can get infected.
Jellyfish or bee sting	Scrape off stinger or tentacles with a flat object, such as a library card. Apply meat tenderizer (to break down the toxin) and ice.

Activity 2: Emergency Telephone Number List

Be prepared for any emergency. Keep a list of important telephone numbers next to the telephone. You can help your family by making your own emergency telephone number list. In this activity, you will need poster board, markers, and a pen. Have a grown-up check your list to be sure all the information is correct. Your emergency phone list should include the following:

- Parents' names and work and cell phone numbers
- Your address and phone number
- Dial 9-1-1 for fire, ambulance, or police emergencies
- Poison Control Center (1-800-222-1222)
- Local police (number)
- Family doctor (name and number)
- List family members with ages and any serious allergies (nuts, bee stings, medicines)
- Nearest neighbor (name, phone number, and address)

Glossary

addicted—dependent on a habit or habit-forming substance.

bacterium (pl. **bacteria**)—microscopic organisms that cause harm inside the body when they multiply and produce toxins

bladder—a baglike organ that stores urine

blood vessel—a tube that carries blood from one part of the body to another

botulism—a deadly form of food poisoning caused by bacteria

contaminated—changed by contact with something bad or harmful (e.g., bacteria)

contract—to tighten

diarrhea—frequent soft or liquid stools (body wastes)

digest—to break food down into smaller parts that the body can use for energy or building materials

esophagus—the tube leading from the mouth to the stomach exhale—to breathe out

fangs—long, pointed teeth, especially the hollow teeth of snakes or spiders that inject poison

food poisoning—an illness caused by eating food that contains certain kinds of harmful microscopic creatures that live and grow inside the body

fungus (pl. fungi)—a plantlike organism that feeds on living or dead matter; includes mushrooms, molds, mildew, and yeast

inflammation—redness, heat, and swelling that develop when tissues are damaged

inhale—to breathe air into the lungs

mucus—a gooey liquid produced by cells in the lining of the nose and breathing passages

organic foods—crops grown without using pesticides or other chemicals

pasteurized—heated to a very high temperature, and then cooled quickly to kill bacteria

pesticides—poisonous chemicals used to get rid of insects and other pests

poison—a substance that can cause sickness or death when it gets inside the body

Samonella—a type of bacteria that can cause food poisoning

toxic—poisonous

toxin—a poison

urine—liquid body waste produced by the kidneys

venom—a poison produced by an animal

vomiting—throwing up; the stomach contents are forced back through the mouth

white blood cells—jellylike blood cells that can move through tissues and are an important part of the body's defenses

Learning More

Books

Acheson, David W. K. and Robin K. Levinson. *Safe Eating*. New York: Dell Publishing, 1998.

Cody, Mildred M. *Safe Food For You and Your Family*. Minneapolis, MN: Chronimed Publishing, 1996.

Kusinitz, Marc. *Poisons and Toxins*. New York: Chelsea House Publishers, 1993.

Latta, Sara L. *Food Poisoning and Foodborne Diseases*. Berkeley Heights, NJ: Enslow Publishers, Inc., 1999.

Scott, Elizabeth and Paul Sockett. *How to Prevent Food Poisoning*. New York: John Wiley & Sons, Inc., 1998.

Skidmore, Steve. *Poison! Beware!* Brookfield, CT: The Millbrook Press, 1991.

Organizations and Online Sites

American Association of Poison Control Centers

http://www.aapcc.org/

This site includes general information on poisoning, poison prevention, and games about poisons.

Arizona Poison and Drug Information Center Home

http://www.pharmacy.arizona.edu/centers/apdic/apdic.shtml

This site has information about poisonous critters, poisons in your home, poisonous plants, poisoning & pets, poison quiz, and more.

Food Poisoning and How to Prevent It

http://www.dhs.vic.gov.au/phb/hprot/food/fhpp/fp1.html

This site includes general information on food poisoning, bacteria and how food gets contaminated, symptoms, and prevention tips.

National Capital Poison Center

http://www.poison.org

This site has general information about household poisons, pet poisons, plant poisons, poison prevention, and first aid treatment.

UCSD Healthcare: Poison: Home

http://health.ucsd.edu/poison/index.asp

This site, provided by the California Poison Control System, has links to information about poisonous plants and animals and first aid.

Index

About the Authors

Dr. Alvin Silverstein is a professor of biology at the College of Staten Island of the City University of New York. **Virginia B. Silverstein** is a translator of Russian scientific literature. The Silversteins first worked together on a research project at the University of Pennsylvania. Since then, they have produced 6 children and more than 180 published books for young people.

Laura Silverstein Nunn, a graduate of Kean College, has been helping with her parents' books since her high-school days. She is the coauthor of more than 50 books on diseases and health, science concepts, endangered species, and pets. Laura lives with her husband, Matt, and their young son, Cory, in a rural New Jersey town not far from her childhood home.